THE
EPSOM
CLUSTER

VOICES FROM EUROPE'S LARGEST PSYCHIATRIC
HOSPITAL COMPLEX

KIRSTIE ARNOULD

AMBERLEY

First published 2019

Amberley Publishing
The Hill, Stroud
Gloucestershire, GL5 4EP

www.amberley-books.com

British Library Cataloguing in Publication Data.
A catalogue record for this book is available from the British Library.

ISBN 978 1 4456 9366 8 (print)
ISBN 978 1 4456 9367 5 (ebook)

Typesetting by Aura Technology and Software
Services, India. Printed in Great Britain.

CONTENTS

ACKNOWLEDGEMENTS

Jeremy Harte of Bourne Hall Museum in Ewell provided the original idea for this book, as well as support, guidance, scanning of photographs and a generous supply of coffee and biscuits during its development. It would not have happened without him and I am enormously grateful. Julian Pooley of Surrey History Centre first introduced me to the extraordinary collection of asylum casebooks in the centre's search room, and has been a source of encouragement, wisdom and practical help in my research. My first encounter with Maud Lipscombe in one of the casebooks originally sparked my curiosity about the missing voices of the Epsom cluster.

The Keeping Us in Mind oral history project was the source of many of the oral histories in this book. It was a partnership between Epsom-based mental health charity Love Me Love My Mind, Bourne Hall Museum and Surrey History Centre, which I led in 2017. Sue Bond, Sarah Dewing, Danielle Grufferty, Kevin McDonnell and Cathy Firebrace all contributed countless hours to researching, interviewing and summarising. Thank you to them.

I am indebted to the Local History Centre volunteers for their research and interpretation work, particularly the content on www.epsomandewellhistoryexplorer. org.uk. Ruth Valentine's fascinating book *Asylum, Hospital, Haven: A History of Horton Hospital* provided some of the details of daily life and a few of the 'voices' of the title. *War Time in a Surrey Town: Epsom 1914–1918* by Trevor White contained invaluable insight into Horton's time as a war hospital. *Tears on My Pillow* by Ray O'Donohue offered a glimpse of Horton in the 1970s and Long Grove in the 1980s. *Memories of Yesterday: A Collection of Reminiscences,* produced by Epsom & Ewell Borough Council Action Group for the Elderly, was the source of additional oral histories.

Most of all thank you to the interviewees who gave their time and their memories to the oral history project. Their generosity has ensured the sometimes opaque story of the hospitals can be illuminated by first-hand accounts.

Almost all the photographs in this book are reproduced by kind permission of Bourne Hall Museum, except the images of Maud Lipscombe, William Collins and Louisa Holliday, which are reproduced by kind permission of Surrey History Centre.

INTRODUCTION

This is Maud Lipscomb, a twenty-three-year-old cigarette maker from Camberwell. She came from a poor family, so it is possibly the only photograph that was ever taken of her. There is no way of knowing if she ever saw it. It was taken when she was

admitted to the Manor Asylum in Epsom on 19 July 1901 suffering, according to her father, from the effects of 'fright and overwork'. She had bruises on the backs of her legs that were unexplained. She refused to answer any questions, saying simply 'I can't tell you' in response.

When she arrived in Epsom it was a prosperous market town in the countryside. The purchase of the nearby Horton estate by the London County Council to construct five asylums for the capital's mentally ill had not been popular with influential local people. The Manor Asylum had admitted its first patients in 1899, and Horton Asylum next door was brand new. Maud was one of over 90 per cent of the asylums' patients classed as 'pauper lunatics', for whom the authorities were expected to care. It is likely that she had never been outside of London; the hospital's grand original manor house and mature landscaped grounds must have seemed like a different world from her life of hardship in South London.

Maud's nineteen years in the Manor take up four pages of a huge leather-bound casebook. To start with, the entries are weekly, then monthly, then annual. They tell the sad story of her gradual decline and how the staff did their best with the minimal treatment that was available at the time. I have not been able to discover what happened to her; she disappears from the records in 1920 when she moved to Horton Asylum, where she may well have spent the rest of her life. Maud was diagnosed with dementia praecox, a term that was used at the turn of the century for what we would now call schizophrenia. It was considered to be incurable, so there was no hope of her ever leaving the asylum.

Maud's image stayed with me for a long time after I read her story. She looks defiant and self-possessed, with an enigmatic half-smile. The picture seems at odds with the description of her removing her clothes and 'throwing herself about' when she first arrived. Was she joking or delusional when she told the staff her head was made of glass? The casebooks describe her as 'noisy', but after she entered the asylum nothing she said was recorded. As one of her nurses wrote, 'little sense can be made of what she says'. No letters or diaries have been found, so Maud's words, and Maud's experiences, are completely lost to us. This question of first-hand experience was the inspiration for this book.

Many of the accounts you find here were collected in 2017 as part of Keeping Us in Mind, a community oral history project funded by Heritage Lottery Fund and delivered in partnership with mental health charity Love Me Love My Mind, Surrey History Centre and Bourne Hall Museum in Ewell. I led this project, which aimed to capture and interpret the stories of those who lived and worked in the hospitals while they were still within living memory.

Keeping Us in Mind showed that the history and meaning of these vast institutions is as varied as the staff and patients who inhabited them. For some people they were a safe haven that provided an opportunity to recover, a place of work where their parents had also earned a living, a source of childhood treats, and somewhere where they socialised, fell in love and met their future spouse. For others they were the location of painful experiences they preferred to put behind them. The experiences of staff and patients were often very different, but they all took place within the same square mile.

This book does not attempt to do justice to the tens of thousands of individual stories and experiences that make up the 100-year history of this unique place. What it does offer is snapshots of a vanished community, and an attempt to place them in a historical context. I have drawn on my own research, and that carried out by others, but you will find there are still many unanswered questions. Research continues and so much of this fascinating history is still waiting to be uncovered.

Susana, an interviewee who grew up in Epsom and whose father worked in the hospitals, said in her interview that the hospitals were always a 'hidden world', behind high concrete walls. These chapters provide a glimpse into that world, an important part of our social history that is rapidly being forgotten. Many official records still exist and are of huge value, but the subjective experiences of individuals are just as significant and more difficult to come by as the years pass.

Since the hospitals closed and were redeveloped for housing there has been no focus for local people to engage with the accounts of people who knew the hospitals, and consider their meaning and legacy. Keeping Us in Mind is, as far as I am aware, the first project that consistently collected and preserved oral histories in audio form from a range of people who knew the hospitals best. This book provides a glimpse into these stories, and I hope that there will soon be a permanent home for them, and for all the research that others have done over the years, in Horton Chapel, the last of the asylum chapels still standing. You can read more about this later in the book.

Since closure and redevelopment the hospital sites are almost unrecognisable, but there are still resonant traces in the landscape if you know where to look. Horton Chapel is one of them, and the final chapter provides some clues to others for those who are inclined to go looking.

A Note About Perspectives

The Keeping Us in Mind project recorded over fifty interviews, mostly with former staff. Only a handful were with former patients. Most had died or moved away, and others were reluctant to share their experiences of a difficult time in their lives, or risk the stigma of admitting to being hospitalised with mental health problems. Staff generally recalled a happy time in their lives, and a thriving community. Some of the patients we were able to interview felt that their stay in hospital had benefitted them, even though it had been painful at the time; others recalled loneliness and isolation. The stories we have collected are important and I am very grateful to everyone who contributed them. As you read, bear in mind that there are other stories, and other perspectives, that are missing from this account.

CHAPTER ONE

ARRIVALS

Epsom is probably best known for its links to horse racing and the Derby. It was the home of Isabella Beeton, author of *Mrs Beeton's Book of Household Management*, and Lord Rosebery, briefly prime minister from March 1894 to June 1895. In the seventeenth century it enjoyed a brief heyday as a fashionable spa town when the healing properties of Epsom Salts were discovered, and Samuel Pepys recorded visiting to take the waters and enjoy the vibrant social scene.

When I moved to Epsom in 2005 that was all I knew about my new hometown. There were some curious features in the landscape nearby – a local park boasted a line of elderly poplars, which I was sure I had read somewhere were planted in country houses and institutions to act as windbreaks. A nearby leisure centre was located in an industrial-looking building of distinctive yellow brick, with what looked like a large, squat chimney. Somebody said it had once been a power station, but it was in an odd location, so far from the town. The north of Epsom, close to where I live, was the site of several new housing estates in beautifully mature landscaped grounds, interspersed with some slightly forbidding older buildings that had been converted into luxury apartments. There seemed to be a semi-derelict church hidden in overgrowth, opposite one of the apartment buildings, which carried an unusually distinguished air. A large brick tower loomed awkwardly among the neat new houses and manicured lawns of the Livingstone Park estate. It was intriguing. I'd been living in Epsom for over a year before I discovered the reason for all this: the new housing estates were being built on the footprint of five psychiatric hospitals, and had retained much of the original landscaping.

The hospitals are an important part of our social history, but as time passes they are fading from memory, as are the people who once inhabited them. The 'Epsom cluster', as the hospitals became known towards the end of their working life, was constructed between 1899 and 1924. It was an extraordinary undertaking; five asylums built within a square mile to house up to 10,000 people experiencing conditions such as dementia, general paralysis of the insane (tertiary syphilis), psychosis, depression, anxiety and the effects of exhaustion, poverty and overwork. Many women were admitted with what we would now term postnatal depression – and released as recovered after a three-month stay – only to find themselves back in the asylum the following year after yet another pregnancy. Sometimes the pattern repeated itself several times. People with learning disabilities and epilepsy were considered to be mentally ill at the time and made up a sizeable proportion of the population of the hospitals. The site was chosen by the London County Council (LCC) to house the capital's growing number of 'pauper lunatics' for whom the city was expected to care, but who could no longer be accommodated in the workhouse or infirmary.

Rural Epsom was chosen as a place in which the urban mentally ill could benefit from the views and fresh countryside; 'the poor man's country home', as contemporary thinking had it. With few effective treatments and the ever-present stigma of mental illness, it also helped that the new institutions could be sited sufficiently far away from the city. Yet thanks to the railway service between London and Epsom families could still visit, and many did so regularly. Their journey from Epsom station would have taken them through 'the lanes', the alleyways that still exist behind Temple Road and between Lower and Upper Court Roads.

The square mile of land around Horton Manor was acquired at a bargain price of £35,900, and the surrounding farmland could be used to support near self-sufficiency in food and all the other facilities that would be needed for what was effectively another town on Epsom's doorstep, including power, sewage and the burial of the dead. The number of on-site facilities required was astounding:

Acute hospital
Cemetery
Bakeries
Cafeterias
Central station to supply water, gas and electricity
Cobbler's workshop
Engineer's offices
Kitchen stores
Laboratory
Laundries
Main stores
Maintenance workshops
Market gardens
Mortuary
Needlework workshops
Pharmacy
Shops
Tailoring workshops
Upholsterer's workshop

A vast workforce was brought in to build the hospitals and another to staff them. Each hospital was like a separate village secluded in the countryside with its own chapel, recreation hall, playing fields and farm. For reasons of economy, and because it was considered to be beneficial to their recovery, the running of the asylums depended on a large, free workforce: the patients themselves.

The cluster's scale was unique in Europe and possibly the world. Planned for 10,000 patients plus staff, it almost doubled the size of Epsom's population and changed the town both geographically and socially. The stage was set for a conflict between the new arrivals and the inhabitants of thriving, respectable Epsom who, after all, had no choice about this sudden disruption to their ordered lives. Lord Rosebery, Epsom resident and briefly Liberal prime minister, led a campaign between 1906 and 1909 on behalf of 'the sane' against walking parties of patients from Horton Asylum in the town. The local press became agitated at the idea of 'lunatics at large!' and of Epsom 'overrun with lunatics'. In 1907 Lord Rosebery went so far as to describe the burgeoning cluster as a 'plague spot'.

However, local tradesmen had a more positive view of the asylums, which were potentially important customers and Lord Rosebery was heckled when he spoke on the subject at a public meeting. The new asylums brought employment for tens of thousands of people over almost a century, many of whom migrated to the area in search of work. Two or three generations of some families worked in the hospitals, and lived in housing nearby on Hook Road, Upper Court Road, Lower Court Road and later in houses on roads such as Horton Hill, just outside the wall that separated Horton Hospital from the outside world. The solid Victorian-designed infrastructure and efficiently planned shared central services for the asylums shaped the local landscape. After a few decades had passed it must have seemed to local people that they had always been there, and always would be. Yet within seventy-five years of the opening of West Park Hospital in 1924 they had all but closed down, their model of care derided and dismissed and their population of staff and patients scattered.

The decline of the hospitals was gradual, although it seemed sudden to many who experienced it. The massive social upheaval set in train by two world wars, a greater understanding of the causes of mental illness, better drug treatments and other therapies and a drive towards the rights of individuals over institutions all played a part. Another consideration was the sheer cost of running such vast establishments and maintaining their buildings and estates at a time when free patient labour was no longer considered acceptable. The hospitals had adapted to the dramatic social, political and medical changes the twentieth century had brought. They started out as asylums, became mental hospitals in the interwar period, and under the NHS were simply known as hospitals like those for the care of physical ailments. Some of their treatments had been considered pioneering in their day. Now they were discarded as no longer fit for purpose.

All five closed between the late 1980s and the early 2000s as a result of government policy to move mental health care out of big institutions and into the community, although some NHS services were retained on the sites at Horton, West Park and St Ebba's. The land was sold to be developed for housing. A century of history met the might of the bulldozer as many of the decaying original buildings built for London's poorest and most needy citizens were demolished to make way for modern homes with all the domestic convenience and comfort expected by inhabitants of the late twentieth century.

When the hospitals closed patients were rehoused under the Care in the Community policy, either in the vicinity of the hospitals or their area of origin. Local people were used to their presence in the town and they seemed to just disappear as one by one the old buildings closed down. Many of the staff, who had come from all over the world, left to find jobs elsewhere. A way of life that had lasted for nearly a century, and seemed as permanent as those solid buildings, came to a sudden end.

The Manor Asylum

In the 1890s, London County Council was struggling to keep up with the number of mentally ill people requiring care in London. Existing asylums were overcrowded and the authorities knew some were dangerous. Colney Hatch Asylum, with its 3,000 patients and temporary timber wards, was understood to be a fire risk well before fifty-two women died in a fire there in 1903.

Ninety-eight per cent of London's mentally ill were termed 'pauper lunatics', so their families were not going to fund their care and cost was a key consideration. The committee who authorised the building would have preferred something rather different as large asylums were already beginning to seem outdated and a smaller, more domestic scale was considered better for patients. In the end though, urgency and the need to keep costs down meant large institutions for up to 2,000 patients seemed the only feasible option.

The Manor Asylum was the first to open, in 1899.

"The Manor"(County of London). War Hospital, Epsom.

One of several postcards of the Manor produced during its time as a war hospital in the First World War. Note the new brick buildings.

When work started on this first asylum at Epsom, the need was urgent and there was no time to wait for a fully functioning facility. Horton Manor house, built in 1712, had been long neglected and was not habitable, so a series of hastily constructed corrugated-iron huts built in the ground had to serve as temporary wards, although brick buildings went up as quickly as possible. Built as a short-term solution, the huts proved sturdy, and some were only finally demolished in the 1950s. The manor house itself eventually became the administrative centre of the hospital and was the first building seen by new arrivals whether staff, patients or visitors. Between August 1916 and April 1919 the Manor was a war hospital, used to treat military casualties. It became the Manor Mental Hospital after the war and from 1922 until it closed it was a hospital for people with learning disabilities.

From 1948, when it was taken over by the fledgling NHS, the Manor prioritised training and rehabilitation, working with moderately disabled young people to help them live in society. Industrial and behaviour therapy at the hospital gained an international reputation.

Therese arrived from Mauritius in the early 1970s to work at the Manor and was struck by its setting and its grandeur: 'My first impression was goodness me it was in the woods! It was so vast.'

Horton Asylum: An Efficient Solution

Horton Asylum was also urgently needed. For reasons of economy and efficiency George Hine, the architect of both Claybury and Bexley asylums, was engaged and

75482.

Horton Asylum opened next to the Manor in 1902.

provided an almost identical design to both those institutions, on a similar 'echelon' footprint, with a long, semicircular corridor linking the wards and administrative areas. Most of the bricks used at Horton were made on-site from a distinctive yellow clay.

During the First World War the asylum was requisitioned by the War Office. Existing patients were moved at astonishing speed to other facilities around London and Horton quickly became a military hospital for servicemen wounded in the war – Horton War Hospital. Its importance and reputation was such that George V and Queen Mary visited in July 1916.

In 1919 it was renamed Horton Mental Hospital and by 1922 there were 1,605 patients, of whom only 187 were men. Those with what we would now term learning disabilities were moved to the Manor to create a new specialist hospital. Before the widespread use of penicillin there was no effective treatment for syphilis, the third and final stage of which was the cause of general paralysis of the insane, responsible for many admissions to asylums. Inducing malaria in patients was found to be effective in halting the progress of the disease, although unfortunately it proved fatal to some who underwent the treatment. In 1925 the Malaria Therapy Unit was established in the hospital's fourteen-bed isolation block.

During the Second World War Horton was again requisitioned as a war hospital, this time treating both military and civilian casualties, and by 1949 it had reopened as an NHS psychiatric hospital. The 1959 Mental Health Act removed the word 'mental'

Nurses Home
County War Hospital, Epsom.
4687.

The approach to the war hospital nurses' home, showing some of the poplars that were planted to shield Horton's exposed site from the weather. This avenue must have been an imposing sight for nurses arriving at Horton for the first time.

from the names of all psychiatric hospitals to provide parity with other medical facilities, and so the former Horton Asylum, briefly Horton Mental Hospital, became simply Horton Hospital.

The hospital closed gradually during the 1990s, and in June 2003 the land was sold for redevelopment as housing.

Ewell Epileptic Colony (later St Ebba's Hospital): A Different Kind of Institution

The Ewell Epileptic Colony, later known as St Ebba's Hospital, was opened in 1903. Radically different in design, it was on a far smaller and more domestic scale than other asylums. It consisted of nine Queen Anne-style villas built around a village green, and originally accommodated 326 patients. More space was quickly needed however, and in 1909 two more villas were built so a total of 429 patients could be admitted.

From 1918 to January 1927 it became a war hospital and later a treatment centre for neurasthenic ex-servicemen. By the end of 1927 it had returned to its earlier purpose, and like the other asylums it had been renamed a mental hospital. Following the Mental Treatment Act in 1930, it became one of the first psychiatric hospitals to treat voluntary patients who had requested treatment rather than being committed

PILEPTIC COLONY,
— EWELL —

w FROM
WATER TOWER   43

A view of the colony from the water tower, showing the very different, much more domestic, style of architecture used for the detached villas.

by doctors. The smaller villas were considered to be much more suitable for this use than large wards. By 1938 the colony had been expanded to 933 beds and renamed St Ebba's Hospital. An innovative adolescent unit was set up in 1949 under the new NHS, for patients between twelve and seventeen years old.

St Ebba's became a learning disability hospital in 1962 and at the same time the adolescent unit moved to Long Grove Hospital. An industrial training unit opened in the late 1960s and by 1979 it was the largest learning disability hospital in the area. When closure was mooted, parents and relatives campaigned for the site to remain a 'village' for people with learning disabilities, but the idea was rejected and in the mid-1990s residents began to be rehomed in the community. A decade later the site was being redeveloped, with a small area retained for long-stay residents.

Long Grove Asylum: American Influences

By the time Long Grove Asylum opened in 1907, modern psychiatric thinking was moving firmly away from large asylums, but yet again the growth in patient numbers and the costs of caring for them meant another Hine asylum was built, to a basic plan similar to Horton. It had beds for 2,149 patients, but reflecting the latest thinking in US asylum design more villas were built in the grounds as well as large wards.

Above and below: These postcards were published by J. G. Tillett of Church Street, Epsom, and posted to an address in Plymouth on 25 November 1907, shortly after the Long Grove Asylum opened.

They were linked by corridors open on one side to the gardens. The idea of connecting the patients to nature was based on sound principles, but sadly the climate did not co-operate and the wind and rain in Epsom meant the corridors were eventually walled in.

Eleven thousand men are said to have been involved in building Long Grove Asylum. A special train was laid on each day from Waterloo to West Ewell and from there the workmen walked to the site. They were paid just before they got back onto the train at the end of the day so they could not make a nuisance of themselves after spending their wages on beer. Ewell had a generous number of pubs and possibly the publicans were less enthusiastic about this policy than other local residents. A light railway was built to transport building materials to the Long Grove site, and later to West Park Hospital while it was under construction; it also served to transfer coal from the station to the central power station, although it never carried passengers.

After the Second World War Long Grove received several hundred Polish servicemen, of whom 300 were still in the hospital in 1951. Ray, who ran the Long Grove social centre in the 1980s, particularly remembered 'The General', one of the approximately

Horton Light Railway, Hollymoor engine, *c.* 1930. Its name survives in Hollymoor Lane, just off Longmead Road.

200 men who were still there in the 1980s, passing the time with games of cards and draughts. Little more is known about them or the reasons they came to Long Grove – historical records relating to mental health are closed for 100 years. Ray commented, 'I wish we'd learned a bit of Polish, because they didn't speak English.'

The hospital closed in 1992 and was redeveloped for housing as Clarendon Park housing estate.

West Park: Delayed by War

West Park Hospital was built between 1913 and 1924. Completion of the work was delayed by the First World War and although many of the buildings were nearly finished when the war broke out, it did not officially open until June 1924. Another large hospital on the basic Hine echelon design, it could accommodate 2,096 patients. Its architecture represented a further development of the American 'colony' design based on smaller accommodation units, but as it had taken ten years to build it did not incorporate the very latest thinking in hospital building, and there were also several large ward blocks.

Some of the original plans have survived, together with a fascinating photographic record of the hospital's construction.

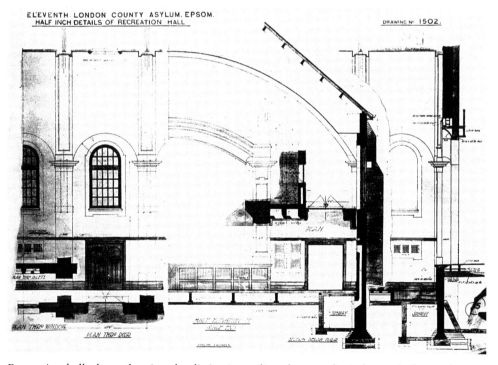

Recreation hall plans, showing the distinctive ceiling shape and windows, similar to those at Long Grove.

Above: The recreation hall under construction in February 1916.

Below: The cafeteria in February 1916.

Above: C and D male wards nearing completion in May 1922.

Below: Construction of ward blocks, with the completed water tower in the background.

Left: The main administration building.

Below: The early stages of the construction of Ramsay Ward, with the completed main administrative building in the background, May 1922.

The main administrative building in the 1980s. It hardly changed in the seven decades it was in use. It has now been redeveloped as apartments.

An airing shelter in the grounds of West Park. These were built in all the hospitals so the patients could enjoy fresh air in all weathers.

These new arrivals in Epsom, so resented by Lord Rosebery, had a lasting impact on the geography of the town and the diversity of its population. An ambiguous relationship between the cluster and the town continued throughout the twentieth century. The hospitals were a major employer and part of everyday life for people who worked in them. Yet they were regarded as separate from the rest of the town and some people say the patients were regarded with suspicion. Some interviewees reported being told by their parents to cross the road if they saw one of the patients coming.

'It was all a bit of a hidden world. There were people who lived on the other side of the long, grey concrete wall. Something happened behind the wall, and then people trickled out and you had to avoid them.' (Susana)

Clive was a neighbourhood police officer in the 1970s and he recalls far more crimes against the patients than committed by them, commenting, 'I was never sure if the wall was there to keep them in or us out.'

Some locals recalled patients being employed in the town and felt that the people of Epsom had been fairly accepting of the patients. Yet unease remained. A small number of former residents with a learning disability lived in sheltered accommodation on the site of the Manor after the main site was redeveloped as Manor Park housing estate. Sue, a former hairdresser at West Park, bought a house there: 'One day one of my friends said, "I'm so scared of the patients" and I was shocked.'

The meaning and legacy of the hospital cluster is, rightly, much debated. For some people who lived and worked in the hospitals, it was a place of purpose, friendship, security and sometimes recovery. Others suffered from, or rebelled against, the constraints of institutional life. You can read a range of views about the closure of the large long-stay hospitals in a later chapter.

CHAPTER TWO

DAILY LIFE

Everyday life in the asylums was just that – at least for the staff. The patients might be experiencing serious mental health issues, but running a huge institution for thousands of patients and managing a vast estate with all the associated services, required ceaseless work from everyone who lived there. The minutes from asylum committee meetings show an increasing preoccupation with the challenges of running the farms and estate as time went

The hospitals were so large, with so many departments, that even staff could have difficulty finding their way around.

on. As intended by the original designers, as much as possible was made or grown on-site. Mostly this was for reasons of economy, but it was also considered to be beneficial for patients to work and morally right that they should contribute to the costs of their care, which would otherwise have fallen on their families. Those who did not pull their weight were judged harshly by the staff; mental illness was no excuse for perceived laziness. There is evidence that patients enjoyed at least some of the work, particularly outdoors. Tim, a groundsman at Horton in the 1970s, remembers working with a small group of patients who volunteered and took a real pride in their work as gardeners.

Entertainment

Entertainment – for both patients and staff – was always a priority and much discussed by the management committees. It was viewed as so essential that each hospital was built with its own grand recreation hall; Long Grove's was particularly admired. These spaces were extensively used for dances, dinners, sports and performances.

Ruth Valentine, in her book *Asylum, Hospital Haven: A History of Horton Haven*, details the varied 'programme of amusements' laid on for both staff and patients in winter 1907:

> Patient's dance and staff dance – fortnightly on Fridays
> Patient's dance – weekly on Fridays
> Sat 5 October – Martin Harvey Dramatic Club
> Sat 19 October – staff concert
> Sat 2 November – 'Butterflies'
> Sat 16 November – Forbes Robertson Dramatic Club
> Sat 30 November – Hampstead Dramatic Club
> Fri 13 December – Annual Ball
> Sat 14 December – Bancroft Dramatic Club
> Christmas Day – Sacred concert in the afternoon

Margaret Nell was a nurse in the Manor in 1943. She recalled:

> On the male side of the hospital there was a sports league. Many patients could play darts, snooker and football. The football team played against other similar hospitals. There was a cinema show and dance each week in the big hall. The leader of the band, which consisted of male nurses, had been resident pianist at the London Palladium. Cash being short he would get a piano part and write it out for each of the other instruments to ensure the band got recent hits.

Sport and entertainment were such an important part of hospital life that many former staff have said that until the 1960s your best chance of getting a job there

Margaret Nell described films being shown at the Manor. The projection room is shown here.

Staff pantomime production at the Manor Hospital, 1928/9. Cast and backstage taken by Frank Woods, photographer and picture framer of No. 1 Waterloo Road, Epsom.

Plays and performances continued to take place in the recreation halls throughout their history.

New year celebrations at Horton in the recreation hall during the 1950s.

West Park recreation hall, seen under construction in the previous chapter, was in frequent – and varied – use.

West Park's recreation hall, virtually unchanged by the 1980s.

The dining hall decorated for Christmas, Horton Hospital.

St Ebba's recreation hall, Christmas 1989.

was if you could play a musical instrument or were good at sport. Serious sporting competitions were held between the cluster hospitals and with other institutions from much further afield.

Helen's mother worked at Long Grove and West Park in the 1950s until she retired in the 1970s. Like many families, hers had been attracted to Epsom from Newcastle just after the Second World War by the promise of work. Her godmother, two aunts and an uncle were all nurses at Horton.

Helen has vivid memories of Christmas parties: '[there was] a huge big staircase (well it seemed huge to me) and I always remember that's the staircase father Christmas came down with his big bag of presents. Every single child had a present with its name on.'

Summer fairs were a highlight for everyone too – children, staff and patients. There was a poignant side to this, particularly for the long-stay patients as Helen remembers: 'We would go on the rides with the patients because they didn't have families to do it.'

Throughout the history of the hospitals, many staff put considerable time and effort into organising parties, days out, holidays and special events for the patients. In the 1970s and '80s the hospital social clubs hosted weekly discos and local residents remember enjoying these and making the most of the subsidised staff bar.

A Horton summer fair was vividly described in one of the local newspapers in 1908:

> one's ideas of what asylum life is like were somewhat upset by seeing the patients having shies, amid hilarious laugher, at the coconuts and at Aunt Sally, indulging – more merriment – in rides on the switchback railway, and on intractable donkeys, and competing with much enthusiasm in sports arranged for their particular benefit.

Albert Tebbs recalled entertainments in the 1950s:

> The two sexes met only once a week on the dance floor and that was under supervision. There was a staff orchestra in the hospital which played during those dances. One of the conditions of employment was that the person could either play an instrument or play a sport, both in order to organise the patients for their activities. There was a cinema show once a week but even that was segregated. My father would get an extra half a crown for running the cinema each Friday and Saturday nights.

Raj and Therese came to the Manor in the 1970s and worked on a ward with young people with learning disabilities. They were keen to provide the people they cared for with events to look forward to: 'At home children have birthday parties. We would have parties for them and we would invite some of their friends from other wards, and we'd invite their parents.'

Ray ran the social centre at Long Grove in the 1980s: '[the patients] came down from different wards they wouldn't mix with otherwise. We used to have a tea bar that would open for an hour. We'd play draughts with them. We had a singing thing once a month. We had a piano there and we'd invite the patients up to sing and dance.

Sports day at St Ebba's, 1980s.

Spiritual life was important, and each hospital's chapel held weekly services for patients. The administration block at Horton is shown here, with the water tower behind. The procession of nurses and clergy are presumably on their way to the chapel, which was opposite the building.

They felt important. We'd clap for them. It was a bit of a London Palladium for them I suppose.'

In the 1980s, Kathleen volunteered on a ward that cared for elderly female patients at West Park. She provided activities the staff did not have time to organise. The ward staff were initially concerned that the visits might unsettle the patients, but in fact both staff and patients came to look forward to the visits.

To begin with Katherine's visits focused on Bible readings and stories and this continued to be important, but over time she recruited a team of volunteers and they introduced other activities. Here she describes one of them: 'We had the Salvation Army there one day – can you imagine the Salvation Army in a ward! We had all the windows open, we had patients from another ward because everyone loves a good sound, don't they?'

A Child's View of the Cluster

Tony's parents both worked at West Park Hospital and he grew up in nearby Ewell in the 1950s and 1960s. He remembers watching the staff travel to work in the early morning, past his house and up rural Horton Lane to work: 'You'd see all these bikes going past from all over Chessington. Probably a hundred bikes. Quite a thing to see every day!'

Tony also recalls sitting on a bridge on Horton Lane with his friends and watching the steam trains on the light railway carrying coal to the central power station.

The hospitals, and the patients, were an important part of his childhood and he remembers his father bringing home beautiful wooden toys with moving parts that had been made by patients in the hospital's workshop. He was also very familiar with his parents' workplace: 'West Park was very open so I went up there many, many times. You didn't see many patients around because they were mostly on the wards, but you did see a few people around and they would say hello and they got to know you.'

Hairdressing

Hairdressing was considered very important, as patients were observed to benefit from taking pride in their personal appearance. Occupational therapists often recommended it as making an important contribution to patients' recovery as it boosted their self-esteem.

Sue worked as a hairdresser for the patients at West Park in the 1980s. She recalls that patients were required to visit the hairdresser whether they wanted to or not. She also remembers the kindness one of the patients showed towards her: 'My nicest memory was when I was pregnant, and one of the patients would wait for me every day while I parked my car and he'd come across the car park with no shoes on, and he'd take my bag and carry it into the hairdressers for me and give me a Marathon bar as he left. He was looking out for me! He didn't say much, but that was what he did.'

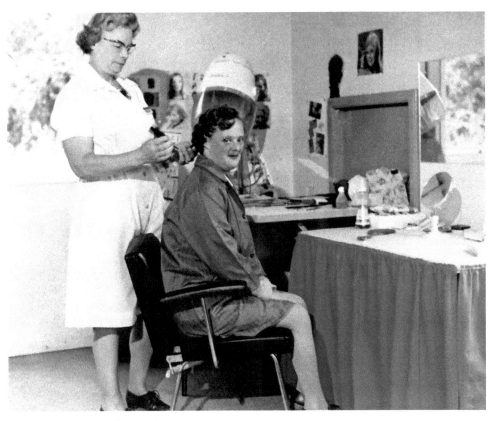

Hairdressing at St Ebba's in the 1960s.

Hairdressing salon at Horton in the 1980s.

Hospital nurseries were essential, as so many of the staff were working parents. The nursery at Horton was opened in 1962. A hairdresser in the hospital salon remembers being offered a nursery place for her son at her job interview: 'That was when I started; my daughter started school, [my son started nursery] and I started work here the same day.'

More Freedom for Patients

As attitudes towards mental illness changed and treatment options improved after the Second World War, new legislation brought greater freedom for patients. The 'walking parties' and organised activities of earlier years had been replaced by patients being trusted to explore the grounds alone where it was deemed to be safe and even go out into Epsom alone.

Peggy Organ was struck by this change when she returned to mental health nursing in the 1970s after taking a break when her children were young: 'When I first went there (in the 1950s) everyone was locked in. We had to count all the patients in and out. When I went back (decades later) I couldn't believe it. The whole place was open; they could do what they liked.'

The patients' rights movement became more influential in the 1970s and nursing training began to reflect these ideas. New recruits often challenged older practices: 'Institutionalisation was seen as a very bad thing, and something that we would be looking out for' (Tracey, trainee nurse at the Manor (1981–84).

'We tried to dress them in normal clothes like you and me, so they didn't stick out. I think the hospital clothes were like a uniform. We had a motto: if it's good for us it's good for them' (Raj, nurse at the Manor).

Corridors

Corridors were a recurring motif in many of the Keeping Us in Mind interviews and they seem to have a multitude of meanings. Some interviewees marvelled at the size of them, others found them frightening and intimidating, particularly as you could hear

An internal corridor at West Park.

West Park external corridor. Originally constructed to be open to the elements, the corridors were eventually glazed. The effect is much less imposing than the enclosed corridors of the hospital's interior.

footsteps well before you knew who was coming towards you in a curved corridor. Of course, they also had an essential practical function and Tim remembers pushing a gang mower down the main corridor at Horton as the most efficient way of moving it around the vast site. In a poignant section of her interview Jacky, former Deputy Director of Long Grove Hospital, mentioned the corridors echoing with the voices of the past as the hospital closed.

A Room of One's Own

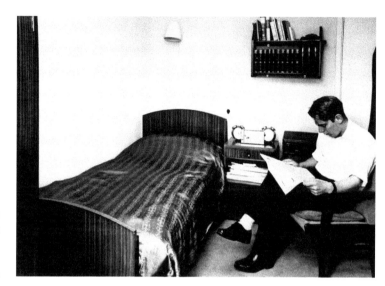

Staff who 'lived in' had only a little more space than the patients, but at least they could benefit from more privacy than a ward offered.

Occupational Therapy

Occupational therapy was a hugely important part of daily life, particularly in the learning disability hospitals, the Manor and St Ebba's. Like the music therapy pioneered at Horton, it allowed patients to learn new skills and express themselves creatively.

Occupational therapy.

Daily Life at Horton

This selection of photographs of Horton Hospital was taken by a staff member between 1981 and 1990. They show some of the staff and patients that made up the hospital's community. There is a sense of camaraderie that was borne out by many of the oral history interviews with staff, although patients did not necessarily see it the same way. As one of Ruth Valentine's staff interviewees put it, 'It was like a family. There never was another hospital like it.'

Resting in the yard.

CHAPTER THREE

WORKING LIFE

As we have seen, Epsom's hospitals employed thousands of staff over the century they were in operation. In the early days the emphasis was on recruiting nurses. Much of the day-to-day work of running of the asylums – growing and cooking food, making and laundering clothes, repairing shoes – was carried out by the patients under supervision. Work kept patients occupied, which was considered to improve their behaviour, and in some cases enabled them to use skills that they had developed

Milking parlour at Horton Hospital. Before the First World War Horton's cows were producing approximately 38,000 gallons of milk per year.

Greenhouses at Horton Hospital in 1989, five years before closure. Once the hospital grew its own food (including 100,000 cabbages a year), but by the late 1960s this had been much reduced.

before they became unwell. For long-stay patients, it ensured they made a contribution to their care. For those who stayed for a shorter time it helped reintegrate them into society.

The farms provided most of the food and their produce was essential to hospital life, so having plenty of free labour was essential. Asylum committee minutes show that milk, eggs, cabbages and even piglets were frequently traded between the different institutions. Presumably they were sent up and down Horton Lane by horse and cart to wherever they were needed.

Evolving Approaches to Nursing

Over time the early model of work changed. Nursing became increasingly professionalised as understanding of psychiatric medicine grew and more treatment options became available, and there was a growing emphasis on ensuring nurses were properly trained. Recruiting staff had always been difficult; the work was hard, the wages were low, and there was a stigma about working with 'lunatics'. The hospitals had long looked beyond the local area for staff. Tim, who grew up in Epsom, told the story of a neighbour who had walked to the town from Norfolk in the 1920s to find work after a relative responded to an advertisement. Eileen Dann's parents were from

Nurses at the Manor at the turn of the century.

West Park nursing awards, 1950s.

Grimsby and Bath. They met at West Park where they were both nurses. They were married in 1929, but had to keep their marriage a secret at work or her mother would have lost her job as married women were expected to give up work.

From the mid-century onwards this recruitment drive intensified and broadened. People were recruited from throughout the UK, and increasingly from all over the world. One of the attractions for nurses was the three-year training programme and the opportunity to develop a new career. There was still a stigma around mental health, but gradually this was changing and the lure of developing professional skills was strong. Nursing was evolving rapidly, from a focus on 'institutional care' to what became known as 'continuing care', with the needs of individual patients at its heart. Nurses helped long-stay patients prepare to leave the hospital, helping them to learn essential life skills like cooking, cleaning and managing their money. One of the wards at Horton, for example, was furnished as a house so long-stay patients could get used to life outside the ward.

Although knowledge about mental illness and treatments were improving, which was making an important difference to patients' quality of life, so much still came down to the relationships between staff and patients. As one Horton nurse with over thirty years' experience commented just before closure, 'A cup of tea and a fag can do more good than 300mg of Sparine [an anti-psychotic medication].'

'Staff From At Least a Dozen Countries': The Cluster's Diverse Workforce

Jacky was Deputy Director at Long Grove when it closed: 'I had staff from at least a dozen countries including China, Malaysia, Iran, Barbados and the Philippines. A brilliant group of people.'

Most staff seem to have welcomed the diversity and to have enjoyed working alongside and learning from people and cultures they might never otherwise encounter. Some elderly patients, though, were resistant to being nursed by people of different nationalities and this could cause tensions on the ward. Cultural differences emerged, too. Tea time was a very important part of institutional life, particularly for older people, and Jacky remembers that patients were not impressed when staff from Asia, accustomed to preparing Chai, added milk and sugar to the teapot before it was served.

During this period the patient population also became more diverse, reflecting the changing demography of London. For example, a 1981 statistical study of an acute female ward at Horton reveals that of the 199 patients, 148 of them described themselves as British and fourteen as Irish. Other ethnic origins were listed as West Indian, Chinese, Hungarian, Filipino, Arabian, American, Polish, Turkish Cypriot, Egyptian, Russian, Belgian, Indian, Greek, French, African and Italian.

In March 1985 John came from North Lanarkshire in Scotland to work at Long Grove, following a friend from his hometown who had made the journey a couple

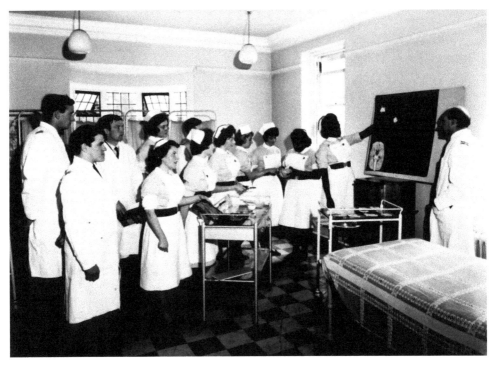

Staff training, Long Grove Hospital, 1960s.

Recruitment publicity image for Long Grove Hospital, 1960s.

of years before and was enthusiastic about life in Epsom. John had no previous nursing experience, but was drawn by the prospect of three years' training: 'I was in the building trade. I worked as a painter and decorator. I worked in places like tyre-fitting, steelworks.'

He was based at Long Grove but undertook much of his training at Horton. The greenery, trees and beautiful landscaping were a revelation. After Long Grove closed, John went on to a career in psychiatric nursing, which took him to France and eventually back to Scotland.

John enjoyed working with colleagues from all over the world. He recalls the importance of 'the international language of food. The Mauritian nurses liked the spices that went into our haggis!'

As many as 40,000 to 50,000 nurses came from Mauritius to work in hospitals in the UK, among them Raj and Therese, who met at the Manor. Raj came to Epsom in 1970, working first at Horton and then the Manor where he met Therese in 1972. They raised their family in Epsom and stayed after the hospital closed.

A Nurse Arrives at Horton

Ray O'Donoghue came to Horton as a nurse in 1971 and his first impressions of the acute male admissions ward were not encouraging: 'The hallway inside the ward was dull and badly in need of decorating. I was even less impressed when I saw six single side rooms, each just about big enough to hold a single mattress on the floor and an old tin locker. On each bed was a patient apparently asleep or drugged up. The doors were obviously locked to contain the patients, and all the rooms were dirty and strewn with garments and newspapers on the unpolished wooden floor.'

Aspects of the regime seemed shockingly old fashioned to Ray after the modern practices he had seen in his previous nursing job, in the pioneering Drug Dependency Unit at Tooting Hospital: 'One of the patients was in a wheelchair but he was also tied to a post. He could walk but I think they put him there to stop him wandering off.'

Ray challenged what he saw as institutionalised practices. He was disciplined on more than one occasion and gained a reputation as a troublemaker. While he was still working at Horton, he started to write a book about his experiences. His note taking was regarded with suspicion by his superiors and he was questioned about his intentions. He left Horton after only two years.

In 1985 Ray returned to the Epsom cluster, this time to work in the Patient's Social Centre at Long Grove. Although he saw the patients most days, he knew little about their histories or conditions. He knew only that most of them had been in the hospitals for decades. Ray talked to them, which the nursing staff on the wards often did not have time to do in the midst of a busy hospital routine. He organised games, music and social occasions to brighten the monotony of a life that, as he saw it, was often broken only by mealtimes and medical routines.

The Changing Role of Work

From the 1960s thinking about the role of work for patients changed and it was considered exploitative to rely on free labour to run the hospitals. There was also an increasing awareness that long stays in hospital could hamper people's ability to function in the outside world, so the role of work came to be seen as rehabilitation of the patient. This meant there was a need to employ staff for roles patients would previously have carried out, and to pay patients for their work in industrial therapy. People came to Epsom to work as porters, domestic staff and in the kitchens. Whole families of siblings came from Italy and Spain, for example, and many stayed, raised their own families in Epsom and made a permanent home here. The result was an astonishingly diverse group of workers as Jacky observed at Long Grove. It also meant that running the hospitals was much more costly than it had been in the days of patient labour, which is likely to have hastened their demise.

For the patients, the change in emphasis from 'earning ones keep' to work as therapy and rehabilitation meant that occupational therapy and industrial therapy became the focus. The tasks could be monotonous, but patients were paid a small amount for their work in industrial therapy. This money could then be spent in the hospital shop, or on visits to Epsom. The cluster began to take on commercial contracts, for example packing cutlery for use on airlines and boxing up Airfix kits. Pupils at nearby Epsom Primary School remember a fire at the nearby Long Grove industrial therapy unit in the 1980s. A group of boys decided to take the day off and acquire as many Airfix

The huge laundry at Long Grove Asylum, where many patients worked until the 1960s. Each hospital had similar facilities.

Above: The machinery might have changed by the 1980s, but not the location.

Below: One of Horton's kitchens shortly after the hospital opened.

A member of staff working in one of Horton's vast kitchens. In the early years this would have been bustling with patients.

The brewery at the Manor Hospital.

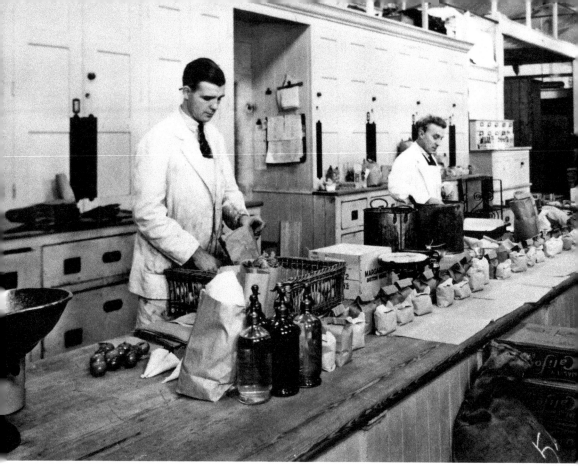

Kitchen stores, Horton Hospital, 1939.

kits as they could before the site was secured. They knew it was dangerous, but the temptation was irresistible.

Without patient labour the farms became less important as more food began to be bought. Many patients – and staff – missed being able to work outside. The hospital grounds were always beautifully maintained but now that walking parties were no longer organised they were not used so extensively. Horton retained a games master into the 1970s but he had little to do; patients were no longer compelled to take physical exercise as part of their routine and many chose not to get involved in organised games.

Workshops

Many of the workshops were still operating in the 1970s, including the bootmakers, tailors, butchers and bakery, as these were seen as valuable places to learn or refresh skills that could be useful in finding a job when they eventually left the hospital.

Horton War Hospital bakery.

Lester Reginald Lee worked as an upholsterer at Horton Hospital. He is in the bottom photograph below, given by S. A. Stage. He was an apprentice at Maples upholsters in London for three years, then moved to Ewell in 1932. Born in 1908, he served in the RAF in World War Two, returning from Africa through Tripoli. He retired from the hospital in the 1970s. The photographs of the workshop show it in operation, with piles of completed goods ready for use in the hospital, or sale.

Albert Tebbs started work at the Manor in 1946 when he came out of the army. His father had stared the brush-making workshop so he worked alongside him: 'There was the brush shop, upholstery, bootmaker, tailor, tinsmith, carpenters and printers. Later on there was also a paint shop. The LCC supplied all the material and the finished work went back to them. Because we could supply the entire needs of the Manor Hospital in a week the rest was surplus.'

In 1965 Albert started Sherwood, a progressive workshop for patients with a learning disability. Sherwood industrial therapy unit produced electrical parts, spot-welding and chain-link fencing, all to commercial standards. The health authority closed the workshop in 1985.

Above and below: Upholstery workshop.

CHAPTER FOUR

WARTIME

'The wounded soldier' said Sir Alfred Keough, Director General of the Army Medical Service, 'has to have the best doctoring, the best nursing and the best treatment that exists in the country.' He was addressing Dr J. R. Lord, who listened closely. It was March 1915 and the army urgently needed facilities for wounded servicemen. Dr Lord, the Medical Superintendent of Horton Asylum, was being given orders to transform his large institution, with its roots in Victorian notions of the treatment of 'lunacy', into a modern war hospital. It was an enormous logistical challenge, but he and his team achieved it.

Horton Hospital, 1916. Patients, nurses, soldiers, and visitors are partaking of refreshments, served from a buffet, in the hospital grounds. The flags hanging from the window indicate a special occasion.

During the First World War 44,613 wounded and sick soldiers from all over the Empire were treated at Horton War Hospital along with many troops from the USA. Almost 20,000 had been wounded in action, with a further 1,200 poisoned by gas.

When the war hospital opened, the local press was enthusiastic about how it had been organised:

A walk around the 17 miles of corridors at the hospital shows what a marvellous institution it is. Ideal arrangements, up to date equipment, in fact everything as it should be for dealing with the wants of the gallant men who are housed there. Everything possible is done to make the boys comfortable and happy, and the entertainments given almost every day are a source of great pleasure to those able to hear them.

On Tuesday 16 July 1916 the king and queen visited the war hospital. They seem to have spent time on most of the wards and spoke to many of the injured soldiers.

Horton's Civilian Patients

In his book about Horton War Hospital, published in 1920, Dr Lord describes how he commanded the military facility with impressive energy and efficiency. He does not describe in detail what happened to Horton's existing patients. They were people drawn from the poorest parts of London and considered too ill – and in many cases too vulnerable – to live in society, so returning them to their families was not possible.

Once Lord received his orders, the asylum was emptied with astounding speed. Over 2,000 patients were moved to other asylums between 12 March and 8 April 1915. Lord's account suggests they were given little more consideration than their meagre luggage – the mass transfer of people, which must have caused some patients great distress, is even termed 'removals' as though they were pieces of furniture. They were provided with a change of clothes only 'where possible'.

This sounds callous to modern sensibilities, but Dr Lord was presenting the realities of his time. Most of Horton's inhabitants were very poor, with few possessions of their own, so as Ruth Valentine explains in her book about Horton, clothing was provided as needed by the asylum from a communal store. They would have been clothed at their destination. Dr Henry Rollin, later Deputy Medical Superintendent of Horton, viewed this period as one of limited resources and inadequate conditions. As for his tone, Lord was writing for his medical contemporaries, who might have expected professional detachment. As commander of a war hospital he reported to the War Office, so unsurprisingly the language of military logistics coloured his writing. There is, thankfully, a hint of empathy. The location of family and friends was considered when patients were moved, so perhaps there were other, everyday acts of kindness and compassion that Dr Lord did not record. One can only hope there were. For the most part, though, his account reflects the position of people with mental illness – at the bottom of society.

Between 25 March and 7 April 1915, 120 female patients from Horton were admitted to the Manor Asylum. It was to be a short stay. In mid-July 1916 the Manor itself was offered to the War Office as a military hospital, and by 11 August more than a thousand patients had been 'distributed' between the other London County Council (LCC) asylums that ringed London, many of which were already overcrowded and struggling to retain staff. Nearby Long Grove Asylum received 120 patients from Horton, but records of the total number of extra patients admitted from other asylums are missing. National figures indicate there was 17 per cent overcrowding in asylums, which makes the doubling of Long Grove's death rate in 1917 and 1918 look disproportionately high.

Sadly the loss of life at Long Grove wasn't unique. On 1 January 1915 the LCC asylums had a population of 21,539 pauper patients. By 1919 there were 17,226. With a bureaucratic shrug of the shoulders, the council's official report laid the blame on 'the high death rate prevailing during those years'. Nationally, asylum death rates rose sharply from 11 per cent before 1914 to over 20 per cent during the war years. Studies have shown that the combined effects of overcrowding, understaffing, poor food and tuberculosis (TB) were probably to blame. During the war patients in asylums were disproportionately affected by a reduced diet compared to the general population, and the unavoidably close proximity to others probably contributed to the spread of TB. At a time of national crisis it seems people suffering from long-term mental illness were not anyone's priority, although the staff undoubtedly did their best under difficult conditions.

Dr Lord went on to enjoy an illustrious career after the war, eventually becoming President of the Medico-Pychological Association. When Horton reopened in 1920 it became Horton Mental Hospital, reflecting the aspirations of a more modern approach to the treatment of mental illness, drawing on the understanding that had been gained in treating servicemen suffering from shell-shock.

Dr Lord used the proceeds of his book to fund the memorial in Horton Chapel to the hospitals 'great and noble purpose' during the war, and to the staff who died, so future generations would not forget. At the time the future of the mental hospital system must have looked as solid as the building itself. Less than a century on, the chapel has been abandoned for almost thirty years and the memorial itself is rarely seen.

Yet during the war years the chapel was central to hospital life; possibly more so than it had been in peacetime. As well as religious services it was used for music concerts on Sunday afternoons, which seem to have been particularly popular with the Australians. There were a number of army chaplains representing denominations from Catholics to the Salvation Army. There was also a rabbi. Almost 5,000 services were held in the chapel, along with some 20,000 communions, over 800 confirmations and twenty-nine baptisms. Funerals were held at the chapel, the first of which were those of Private Riley and Private Leach. After the service, the cortege travelled through a silent Epsom to the military cemetery in Ashley Road.

The Revd. D. Jenkins died in 1919 of influenza caught while at Horton caring for the sick. The same epidemic claimed the lives of many medical staff – Captain Philip

Frith postcard of the chapel during the war. An altar screen and memorial plaques were added in 1920, funded by the proceeds of Lord's book.

Roll of Honour, Horton Mental Hospital.

Fergusson, a surgeon from Manchester and eye specialist, who had joined the Royal Army Medical Corps on the outbreak of war; Daisy Martin, who had left a job as a parlour maid to qualify as a nurse; Lydia Foyan, another probationer nurse; and Grace Libby, Head Land Girl. All these people are commemorated on the plaque to the War Hospital dead beside the chancel steps, which is currently being restored as time has taken its toll and the names are very difficult to read. On the other side is a plaque to the LCC staff who left Horton Hospital to serve their country and never returned.

Scenes from Horton War Hospital

Mr A. G. Brown remembers:

I used to visit the hospital a lot – my father was working there. I had a personal interest in two of the wounded. One was my cousin Ernie Brown and his coming raised a special cheer when he came off the hospital train. He was the very efficient goal-keeper from the town football team. As soon as we lads in Pound Lane spotted the train slowly puffing up past the farm we used to dash up to West Hill. The siding was just by the bridge in West Street and it was there that the wounded were put into Ford ambulances driven by young ladies.

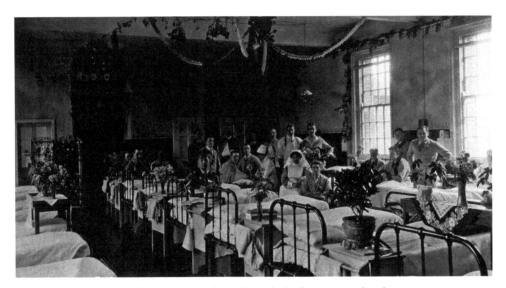

A ward in Horton War Hospital. Note how close the beds are to each other.

Staff photo, Horton War Hospital.

A view of a ward block.

There is quite a contrast between the official hospital photographs used on postcards, which show off the building, the grounds, and scenes of order and efficiency, and the pictures of life in the war hospital that the staff and patients thought worth recording – like this snowball fight.

Above and below: These postcards of the war hospital were produced by local photographers and sold to convalescent servicemen.

Between the Wars

After the First World War both Horton and the Manor returned to their function as psychiatric hospitals, but with new names: Horton Hospital and the Manor Certified Institution (later the Manor Hospital). The changes of name were imposed nationally, but they seem to have reflected a change in attitude towards mental illness and a growing understanding and acceptance that if brave soldiers could be affected by shell shock, it was not a sign of weakness. From 1918 to 1927 the Epileptic Colony became the Ewell War Hospital. It was one of the few hospitals dedicated to the treatment of servicemen who had been both physically and psychologically affected by the war. This represented a major change in the approach to the treatment of mental illness as it gave parity to mental and physical conditions, and showed a new optimism that treatment could actually play a role in full recovery and a return to a full life outside the hospital.

A War Hospital Once More

During the Second World War, Horton was one of only five hospitals in the country to be cleared of its civilian patients to serve the war effort. It became an Emergency Medical Services Hospital, ready to take both military and civilian casualties. Four hundred patients were moved from Horton to West Park in two days. Air-raid shelters were built and gas masks distributed. West Park also became the temporary home of the central pathology lab at the renowned Maudsley

Prepared for everything, including the very real risk of incendiary attack, with the hospital's own fire engine.

Land girls on Horton Farm. John, who trained at Horton in the 1980s, recalls that one of the former land girls still lived and worked on the farm.

Resting in the grounds of Horton War Hospital. The blankets and bare tree indicate this was taken in the winter, so the air must have been very fresh indeed on Horton's exposed site.

Psychiatric Hospital in South London. A dramatic increase in mental illness among the civilian population as a result of the prolonged bombing of London was expected, but never materialised.

From Ireland to Epsom: A Nurse's Story

Elizabeth McDonnell (née Keogh) came from Ireland in the early 1930s. She studied nursing at St Stephens's Hospital in Chelsea and passed her exams at the first attempt. She planned to specialise in midwifery, but just before war broke out she and some other probationer nurses were told they would be working at another hospital and transported to Epsom by coach.

> From the windows of the coach the view seemed like heaven after London. Lush green lawns, flower beds, trees, peace, birds singing, beauty and tranquility. Before we could get off the coach the air raid sirens sounded an alarm! We quickly got off our coach, donned our gas masks as instructed and were led crocodile fashion into the hospital interior. Eventually the "All Clear" sounded. We never did find out what had caused the sirens to sound the alarm. Horton became my home until the end of the War.

Elizabeth worked mostly on the military side of the hospital, and was surprised that the early months of the war were relatively quiet. In the warm early summer of 1940 some of the nurses on night duty were sleeping on the balconies during the day when they were woken by military vehicles: 'Our first casualties from Dunkirk had arrived. On my ward we had thirty to forty soldiers. As the senior nurse on my

LONDON COUNTY COUNCIL HORTON HOSPITAL EPSOM

ROLL OF HONOUR 1939-1945
IN MEMORIAM

CATES, ALFRED	LANCE BOMBARDIER	ROYAL ARTILLERY
GREENSLADE, JOHN LEONARD	T/CORPORAL	ROYAL AIR FORCE
JAMES, GEORGE RICHARD	LANCE CORPORAL	EAST SURREY REGT
ROBERTS, ALBERT	PRIVATE	ROYAL NORFOLK REGT

ward one of my responsibilities was to collect and collate the information about every patient admitted. This information had to be with the Night Superintendent by midnight. My ward was full of French soldiers! They spoke almost no English and I just had schoolgirl French. Thankfully, a student doctor spoke fluent French and was able to help.'

Soon after Dunkirk civilian patients affected by the Blitz began to arrive, and nurses were deployed to the civilian side of the hospital: 'One of the patients that we had was a lady who, heavily pregnant, had been walking through a park when she was caught in an air raid. She suffered a badly broken femur but her baby was unharmed and was successfully delivered. I remember hearing that when the lady had been brought in she was very concerned to have lost her glasses. The ambulance driver went back to the spot where she had been found and discovered her glasses in the lower branches of a tree!'

While she was at Horton, Elizabeth attended services in the chapel, where a roll of honour was installed after the war.

CHAPTER FIVE

PATIENTS' EXPERIENCES

I am; yet what I am none cares or knows;
My friends forsake me like a memory lost;
I am the self-consumer of my woes: They rise and vanish in oblivious host,
Like shades in love and death's oblivion lost;
And yet I am, and live with shadows tost...

John Clare

The Keeping Us in Mind oral history project was started partly with the intention of allowing former patients to speak for themselves. Those who shared their experiences contributed an enormous amount to our understanding of life in the hospitals, but we are aware that they make up a small proportion of our interviews. There are many other stories that have not yet been heard. Many experiences remain untold, or are only glimpsed in the accounts of others. The number of patients we were able to interview has been limited partly because many were elderly when the hospitals closed. Sadly, long-term mental illness can shorten someone's life expectancy by up to twenty years. Some people contacted us but did not want to relive a distressing time in their lives by recording an interview. Others still felt stigmatised by the experience. The silences and absences of the past both reveal and conceal.

Throughout the history of mental health care it has been hard to capture the direct experience of patients. The casebooks at Surrey History Centre can provide glimpses of these stories, and two are shared here. Both are from the early days of Ewell Epileptic Colony.

They are filtered through the prevailing views of the time, and the subjective judgements of the medical staff, but it is still possible to glimpse something of the patient's personality and how they responded to their surroundings.

Louisa

On 8 September 1903 Louisa Holliday was transferred from Bexley Asylum to the newly opened colony. She was nineteen years old and had started experiencing seizures three

years previously. The latest attack had lasted nine months. She had left school at the age of twelve and had been able to earn her own living as a domestic servant until she was sixteen. What happened after that is unclear, but she spent periods in several infirmaries in East London. She had been diagnosed with syphilis the year before she arrived in Ewell.

On admission Louisa was threatening suicide. Clearly frightened, she was described as 'very noisy, constantly shouting and crying loudly'. Hauntingly, she thought men were coming into the ward during the night at Bexley. This was dismissed, but what if it were true? After all, her doctors did not consider her to be delusional. When she arrived at Ewell she was diagnosed with 'epileptic imbecility'.

There were hints that she had been violent at Bexley, but she was considered to be sociable and willing to work when she entered the colony. Sadly, however, these first impressions didn't last. By 14 September she was described as 'unstable' and 'unruly'. She experienced frequent fits; on one occasion forty were recorded in twelve hours. The casebook states 'she is prone to make unfounded accusations'. A nurse wrote that she said money had been stolen from her. Perhaps it had been. Certainly she sometimes became very angry, swearing and on several occasions hurling chamber pots at the nurses. Often in pain from a gastric condition, Louisa frequently took to her bed when she wasn't sent there for disturbing the other colonists. Consequently, she was described as 'lazy' and 'of little help in the institution'. Furthermore she was described in her official medical record as 'a nasty, disagreeable, mischief-making girl'. The type of pejorative language used to describe the early patients could still be found in their notes in the 1980s, as trainee nurse Tracey found at the Manor that 'Many of the [older] patients had really strange diagnoses. You would look in their notes and somebody would be "feeble-minded", for instance.'

Although Louisa only weighed a little more than 6 stone she seems to have been considered threatening. She spent 7 and 8 November in seclusion in the padded room. On 20 March 1905 she was in there again, apparently for threatening a nurse, although it is possible she was also placed there to keep her safe during her fits.

Was Louisa just too troublesome for the colony? It is impossible to know, but after many complaints from the staff about her behaviour she was abruptly transferred back to Bexley on 22 March 1905, after only eighteen months in Ewell.

William

William Collins seems to have had plenty to say for himself. He was admitted to the Epileptic Colony in August 1908 after apparently suffering an epileptic seizure while in Brixton Prison for petty theft. He talked openly about his past and his family, cheerfully describing his father as a 'drunkard'. He seems to have tried the patience of the staff, both with his incessant chatting and his lack of repentance for his crime. He told an extraordinary story about simulating suicide by poison in Richmond Park in order to frighten his 'sweetheart' after an argument. Someone called the police and he spent a few weeks in Brookwood Asylum after this incident.

Almost immediately after he was admitted he started saying that he had never had a seizure and had only pretended to have one in prison. He seemed to enjoy life at the colony, which presumably was easier than making ends meet through petty crime. He was described as 'well-behaved', and managed to make himself very useful working in the kitchen in Pine Villa. He let it be known he wanted to stay, but unsurprisingly by 5 December he had been identified as a malingerer and recommended for discharge. The game was up. Taking a cautious approach, the hospital committee decided that as he had previously spent time in Brookwood he should be discharged for a four-week trial to ensure he was not actually experiencing mental illness.

William seems to have become impatient with waiting for his relatives to come and collect him and took matters into his own hands. At 7:15 on 17 December, 'The door of the villa was left open by an attendant to allow Collins to refill a scuttle of coal. He had previously secreted his boots in the coal yard and having slipped them on in place of his slippers bolted away into the grounds. His absence was noted almost immediately, but a search failed to find him.'

No further attempt seems to have been made to track him down beyond the hospital grounds. In accordance with the law of the time, patients could be discharged after seven days if they were not found, and the asylum formally washed its hands of William fourteen days after his escape. At a time when there was no voluntary admission to hospital, it was not unusual for patients who had been committed to the asylum to flee detention. By the 1920s up to twenty-four people a week were escaping across the country.

Sheila

Padded rooms like the one Louisa experienced were still in use much later in the twentieth century. Sheila was a patient at Horton Hospital twice during the 1960s. Here she describes her first admission:

> This was the first time I'd ever been unwell in that way. When I got to the hospital I was put in a lock-up ward. I was aware it was a mental health hospital and I was running up and down the ward in agitation until somebody sedated me. When I first came in I think I was put in a padded cell. There was just a mattress on the floor, nothing else.

The padded room at Horton.

Hazel

Hazel was a patient at Horton in 1987. 'I experienced life at Horton as it was beginning to close little by little. The whole site gave the impression that time had no meaning, past met present, met future. Time and space to take stock before moving on with the hurly burly of modern life.

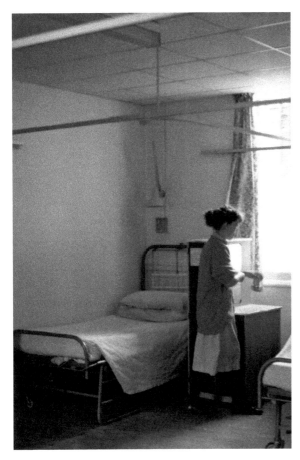

Ashford Ward, West Park Hospital
(taken by Pat Spicer, who was a
nurse at the hospitals for thirty-three
years). It shows the limited space
available for patients like Hazel,
and the sparseness of the ward
environment.

Life was hard there at times, there was prejudice and misconceptions and personal pain. My locker and my bed my only true space, but I feel privileged to have known life at Horton for the space of a year.'

Tracey's and Brian's Accounts

Many interviewees recalled a lack of privacy and dignity in institutional life. The picture overleaf was taken around 1910, but Tracey described a similar scene at the Manor in the 1980s when she was a first-year student nurse, although she only witnessed this once and it is difficult to know if it was common practice. 'There were all these men. Naked and semi-naked. Some were lined up around an open area of baths. I tried to supervise the bathing. No-one batted an eyelid.'

Tracey was shocked by this incident, but this was not the whole picture. Many staff were very caring towards their patients and certainly by the 1980s staff were being trained in how to challenge and address institutionalisation. It was not easy when the hospitals had been built with Victorian ideas of how to address mental health in mind,

Some communal washing facilities were still in use in the 1980s.

and the whole infrastructure had been designed to promote behavioural cohesion and communal living rather than individualised care.

Some long-term patients had become institutionalised and chose not to interact with those around them, but there were occasional breakthroughs. Brian was a nurse at West Park and remembers taking a patient who very rarely spoke for a walk. Out of nowhere, the patient named every tree in the grounds: 'I looked up his record and he'd been a gardener. I never knew. It was quite a revelation.'

Mandy

Mandy recalls some of the children at the Manor waking up in the night hungry because they had not been given enough to eat at mealtimes: 'Some of the food was absolutely disgusting. It was all slushy. It wasn't normal portions, like baby portions and all mashed up as if was baby food. They gave you a spoon and fork every time instead of a knife and fork. Trying to cut the little sausages up – it was awful. One sausage – not two. Sometimes children like two!'

Mandy was admitted to the Manor in the 1960s as a child of six or seven. She found it a lonely experience: 'I used to be left on a little ward traipsing up and down in a little corridor on my own. There was no-one to talk to.'

A member of the domestic team in the 1970s has similar memories of children begging her 'Lulu give me bread'. It put her job at risk, but she always did.

Ray recalled that in Horton in the 1970s adult patients were limited to two slices of bread. He got himself into trouble with the hospital authorities for giving patients bread whenever they were hungry.

The idea of food being so restricted as recently as the 1970s is surprising, but there were reasons – historical, practical and cultural – for all this thrift. The cost of running such vast institutions was enormous, budgets were always tight and economy had to be observed in food as in other areas like clothing. From the very start, asylum minutes show that close attention was paid to food rations for the patients and these were strictly observed. Louisa Holliday's casebook, for example, firmly states that her care is 'chargeable to Lambeth'. The colony was not going to pay for anything that was someone else's responsibility.

Dan

Dan was admitted to the Adolescent Unit at Long Grove in the 1980s. He is now a university professor in Canada. 'The best thing that ever happened to me was being a patient at Long Grove. It made me aware of the fragility of life, the reality of mental health for everyone.'

The treatment Dan received, together with the long-term support of his family, meant that he was able to pursue a career and lead a fulfilling life, although sadly he found out later that this wasn't the case for all his contemporaries. Cuts to mental health care in the UK concern Dan deeply. He questions, 'What would my options be now if I was 15 and in the same scenario?'

Electro-Convulsive Therapy

ECT (Electroconvulsive Therapy) is a treatment that involves sending an electric current through the brain to trigger an epileptic seizure to relieve the symptoms of some mental health problems. The treatment is given under a general anaesthetic and muscle relaxants are given to prevent convulsions.

No one is sure how it works, but anecdotal evidence from some patients (and results of clinical trials) suggest it is often successful when other treatments have failed. Until the 1970s it was used far more than it is now, without anaesthetic and often without consent. It remains a controversial treatment, partly because of this troubling history. (Source: MIND website)

'There were two or three of us having ECT in the same room, with the beds close to each other. They just took me along and put me down on a bed and I suppose gave me some sort of anaesthetic.'

The treatment was not explained to Sheila, and there was no warning it was going to happen: 'When I came to I got some short-term memory loss. I didn't like this. I think it happened two or three times, but I used to try and avoid it by drinking water so that they couldn't give it to me.'

CHAPTER SIX

CLOSURE AND AFTERMATH

Horton's water tower was much climbed by urban explorers after the hospital closed. Although it had been proposed as the centrepiece of a memorial garden, residents of Livingstone Park became concerned about their safety because of its poor state

The Horton water tower, described as 'brutalist' by a former employee.

of repair before the scheme could be developed. It was demolished in early 2012. Many local people, like Tim, who worked in the grounds at Horton in the 1970s, were glad to see it go. Tim described it as 'brutalist' and regarded it as a symbol of the institution's power and control over patients;

> There they stand, isolated, majestic, imperious, brooded over by the gigantic water-tower and chimney combined, rising unmistakable and daunting out of the countryside – the asylums which our forefathers built with such immense solidity to express the notions of their day. Do not for a moment underestimate their powers of resistance to our assault...

On 9 March 1961 the Rt Hon. Enoch Powell, Minister of Health, delivered an address to the National Association of Mental Health's annual conference. He outlined a new government policy that was, to many in the audience, unthinkable: change the entire model of mental health care and close the outdated institutions that, as the government of the day saw it, struggled to accommodate new approaches. At one stroke he identified a mundane part of hospital infrastructure with all that was wrong with institutional care.

The policy was based on evidence, however. New psychiatric drugs were introduced in the 1950s, and the number of long-term patients rapidly started to reduce. Many people could manage their own medication and did not need to be in hospital, or could be admitted for a relatively short period. The idea of care in

'Hospital building is not like pyramid building, the erection of memorials to endure to a remote posterity' (Enoch Powell, 1961). For many staff it seemed impossible that the hospitals, with their monumental air of permanence, their vast physical and human infrastructure and their sense of community, could ever close. The imposing architecture, like the administration block at Horton seen here after closure, with the water tower behind it, intimidated some patients and staff, but provided a sense of security for others who spent decades living and working here.

Above and below: As parts of the hospitals closed they were sealed off and boarded up. Once busy offices, workshops and living spaces became empty and silent, giving an eerie and neglected feel to parts of the sites. There were fewer people around now. Large numbers of staff were made redundant and found work elsewhere or returned to their home countries, and patients were moved to other institutions or out into the community.

Above: Poignantly, even once-lively play areas were abandoned, as staff members and their families moved away.

Right: West Park corridor after closure. 'I remember going in [to work] one autumn evening, and the leaves were now being blown around the corridors. Walking down these corridors it felt like it was echoing with the voices of the past, with people who used to walk down the corridors and say "hi" and greet you' (Jacky, Deputy Director of Long Grove at the time of closure).

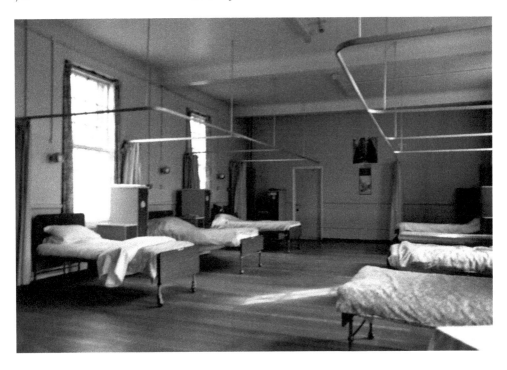

Above: It seems surprising now that people could live on wards for decades, with so little privacy and with just a locker and a bed to call their own. Yet Sue, a former mental health social worker who was involved in rehoming long-stay patients from West Park, recalls an elderly woman who was distressed at being moved off the ward where she had lived for decades. She was frightened to be in a private room on her own, and wanted to sleep near her friends as she always had.

Left: Once the land and buildings were sold, pragmatic decisions needed to be made about what remained and what would be demolished and replaced with modern houses and apartment blocks. The developers were required to retain most of the landscaping, and the handful of listed buildings, and only build on the footprint of the original hospitals. This undoubtedly helped to retain the character of the conservation area and its precious green spaces.

the community took hold, a policy that aimed to support people with a mental illness or learning disability to live their lives in society like anyone else. There was a growing realisation about how costly such big institutions were, and that they were likely to become even more expensive. They took huge numbers of staff to run, and not just medical staff. Maintaining such a large and elderly estate looked unsustainable, particularly once the use of patient labour was phased out. Closure began to seem inevitable, but it would be many years before the policy was fully carried out; in 1971 there were still 1,438 patients at Horton.

While patient numbers declined, hospital life continued much as it always had. Tim, who worked at Horton in the 1970s, observed that for many of his colleagues, 'The hospital became their village.' Food and accommodation were provided and entertainment laid on in the form of sporting competitions, social clubs and discos. Staff met their husbands and wives at work, socialised with colleagues and raised their families in hospital housing. It was not unusual for two or three generations of the same family to have worked in the cluster hospitals.

Closure had been talked about for years, but it was difficult to believe it would actually happen. To long-standing staff, when closure came it seemed very sudden, and the emotional impact was enormous. Jacky was Deputy Director at Long Grove when it closed. She has vivid memories of that time: 'The whole hospital was full of grieving, bereaved people. In my mind I sometimes likened it to the closure of the coal mines, and the break-up of a whole community.'

The buildings that were retained were those that could become attractive homes and were structurally sound. Even when this was the case substantial work needed to be done. Roof timbers, like these at the Manor, were replaced before the building could be converted.

For Dan, who had vivid memories of the Long Grove adolescent unit in the 1980s, the redevelopment of the sites was nothing less than an obliteration of their memory and meaning. He recalls visiting Clarendon Park, on the site of Long Grove. Looking for a building he remembered, 'I went desperately looking for it. My memories of the place were pretty strong, visceral. I knew exactly where I was, where I had to turn. The light was fading and I knew I wouldn't have much more time left. I vaulted a fence, waded out through a field, found a bridleway which was beyond it, double-backed through and found a few cornerstones of bricks. That was the most accurate reflection of what had happened to that site. Never mind all the BMWs and triple-glazing, it was the corners of bricks that really were the true representation.'

Fire at Long Grove

On the night of 22 September 1993, shortly after Long Grove closed, the magnificent recreation hall, seen below, was completely gutted by fire. Whether it was arson or an accident is not known, but Dr Henry Rollin, former Deputy Medical Superintendent at Horton, saw it as symbolic. Writing in the journal *History of Psychiatry*, he said, 'The inferno, literally and symbolically, brought to a tragic and inglorious end a hospital with a long and proud tradition of excellence.'

The magnificent recreation hall at Long Grove before the fire.

Above left, above right and below: Images showing some of the damage after the fire.

Urban Exploration: The Cluster's Gothic Afterlife

Once the hospitals closed they drew the attention of urban explorers, who usually visited by night and played cat and mouse with the security guards to gain entry. The lure of decaying grandeur, and of Gothic fantasies about what had happened in the asylums, proved enduring. Many thousands of the images they took can be found on the internet. The mortuary and padded room at West Park had particular appeal, as did the nursery, which was misidentified as a children's ward.

Perhaps they found something apocalyptic in the ruins of these vast institutions, which had once seemed so permanent. The photographs are eerie, often showing furniture and curtains left intact, and people's possessions still in cupboards and storerooms. Many are also very beautiful. Once roof tiles were removed paint, wallpaper and plaster began to peel off in delicate, discoloured filigree patterns. High sash windows reflected in melancholy pools where dayroom floors were carpeted by water.

West Park's Dartford Ward after closure.

Dartford Ward.

What Happened to the Patients?

The buildings were the most visible symbols of closure, but they were not the most important aspect of this far-reaching change. Enormous efforts were made to rehome people to the most suitable location, working with their families wherever possible. Sometimes this was independent living, or a small group of people would be housed together, with support. By the time the hospitals closed, most of the long-stay patients were elderly and often a residential care home was the best option for them, but it was a difficult transition. Both Jacky and John recall that a significant number of the elderly long-stay patients at Long Grove unfortunately did not live for very long after they left the hospital. Mark, who was one of the social workers who helped rehome people, commented, 'Perhaps we didn't hear the voices of the people saying, "I'm seventy, I've been living here for fifty years. Can't I just have a few years more?"'

However, outcomes were much better for some other people: 'I asked one man what it was like to leave and I expected him to say, "Oh it was really hard, I really missed it." But he just smiled and said, "it was very … pleasurable."' (Sue, former Social Worker)

The Legacy of Closure

The impact of the closure, and of Care in the Community, continues to be debated. Most of our Keeping Us in Mind interviewees felt that, as Mark commented, 'there was a good reason why we did the closure' and that for most people, living in the community is a much better option than a large institution. However, opinions differ on what was gained and lost when the hospitals closed, particularly as the care and support that was actually in place failed to live up to the original aspirations.

Jeremy was a social worker at Long Grove in the 1980s. Working for an organisation called Mental Health Aftercare Association, he helped long-stay patients to find new homes with families, with the idea that they would eventually live independently. He later went on to lecture in social work at the University of Kingston: 'The idea of community care is heroic, brilliant … but there is a thing called reality.'

Tracey was a student nurse at the Manor in the 1970s, and a went on to a career in learning disability nursing. 'Nowadays people with learning disabilities are very isolated and unsupported.'

Susana, Epsom resident: 'People said "I don't mind where they go, as long as they're nowhere near me."'

Dan, former patient: 'A group of people who were lost to society had their safety nets cut and had to survive on their own.'

Mandy, former patient: 'I had some bad times and I had some horrible times [in the Manor] … but in a way it's a shame it's gone because a lot of people moved to lots of places. A lot of people loved the Manor.'

Horton Chapel: Bringing the Past into the Present

Horton Chapel is the only chapel of the cluster that was not demolished, and until recently its future looked uncertain.

When Horton Asylum was built, religious worship was considered an important consolation for people experiencing mental illness, and each hospital had its own chapel. Horton's was built to accommodate 1,000 people – roughly half the inmates. However, eight years after the hospital opened, in 1909, only a third of patients attended services. By 1922 the number had fallen to below a fifth.

During both wars it was used by servicemen of all faiths for both religious services and concerts. 'The services were attended by patients and staff and were always well attended. Catholic services were held by a priest from Saint Joseph's church in Epsom. My eldest son lives in Epsom; when his daughters were small the chapel was still being used as a place of worship and we would sometimes go there for Mass on a Sunday morning.' (Elizabeth McDonnell, a nurse at Horton War Hospital)

In 1961, just as Enoch Powell was declaring the end of the asylum system, this chapel in the shadow of the water tower gained a new purpose. A wall was built in the centre, and half the chapel became Harewood Hall, a music therapy centre complete with Steinway grand piano, named after Princess Mary, Countess of Harewood, who opened it. She was the daughter of George V and Queen Mary, who had visited Horton in 1916. Lady Harewood Way, on nearby Clarendon Park, commemorates her contribution to the hospital's history.

Music therapy at Horton had been championed by Dr Henry Rollin, Deputy Medical Superintendent, who went on to a distinguished career. A woman's choir was formed, as well as a percussion band, jazz and chamber music and concerts were held. As Rollin said, 'perfection was not aimed at and certainly not attained; but what was achieved was a psychological triumph for performers and audience alike'. By 1961 some 200 patients were taking part in music therapy sessions at Horton.

The organ's beautifully decorative pipes came from Winchester College in 1903.

Long Grove's chapel during demolition, showing the red-brick and Gothic arches more typical of asylum chapels than the classical arches of Horton Chapel.

On 12 December 1961, the *Daily Telegraph* reported:

> The hospital's deputy medical superintendent, Dr Henry Rollin, who is himself a music lover, said that the patients originally chosen for these groups had resisted all acknowledged forms of treatment.

> It was soon found that these patients, normally silent, apathetic and asocial, could be persuaded to join in vigorously with a forceful rhythm played on the piano – the success of the performance being judged from the volume of complaints from neighbouring buildings and offices.

> For the first time, in fact the patients began to show signs of animation using music as a means of communication instead of words.

Horton Chapel escaped demolition because it was a Grade II listed building, but after closure it proved difficult to find a viable plan for its future. It remained empty for three decades, the fabric of the building slowly deteriorating. Despite security measures vandals

Above: Shown here in the 1980s, the chapel stood proudly opposite the main administration building, serving its dual function as a place of worship and music therapy centre. Today the windows and doors are boarded up and it is enclosed by a chain-link fence, but a revival of its fortunes is imminent.

Left: The chapel's landscaped grounds, shown here in the 1980s, have become very overgrown in the last three decades, but will shortly become a garden for the new arts centre.

broke in, using the old service tunnels that had heated the chapel when it was built. They smashed windows and light fittings and destroyed the organ – although fortunately the magnificent organ pipes remained undamaged. In 2016 a group of local people formed a charity with the purpose of saving the chapel, and converting it into an arts centre, a vision entirely in keeping with its thirty-year period as a music therapy unit. It will house a permanent exhibition about the cluster hospitals. Local interest and support has been overwhelming, and open days where the public can view the chapel's interior have proved very popular. The centre will open its doors in 2020, and this remnant of the 'hidden world' of the hospitals will enable future generations to discover a fascinating and important part of Epsom's history.

'It's a story that needs to be told.' (Dan, former patient).

CHAPTER SEVEN

TRACES IN THE LANDSCAPE

The north of Epsom has avoided urban sprawl, and this is largely because of the legacy of the hospitals with their farms and landscaped grounds. The green space, which is so highly prized by those who now live on the new estates, was designed to promote recovery in those who came to Epsom as patients; an antidote to the stress of poverty and urban living at a time when treatment options were limited. In the twenty-first century, wellbeing is boosted for everyone in the area who can enjoy walks and cycle routes around the old hospital sites, and through Horton Country Park, which was once farmland, and part of the route of the light railway.

Most of the square mile that was once covered by the hospital cluster has been redeveloped for housing, and new roads and routes around the site have been constructed. Yet the old asylums have left their mark. Perhaps understandably the developers chose not to name the estates after the hospitals with the exception of the Manor, which is now Manor Park; Horton became Livingstone Park, Long Grove is Clarendon Park, St Ebba's Parkviews and West Park is now Noble Park. Road names reflect the area's history: Hine Close on Livingstone Park, for example, is named after George Hine, who designed Horton, Long Grove and West Park. When I visited the former Long Grove site with John, who had been a nurse there in the 1980s, he was pleased to see that the names of the first wards he worked on were retained at Hunter and Harvey Court.

The developers were permitted to build on the footprint of the original buildings and had to retain as much as possible of the original landscaping, so Hine's distinctive echelon design can still be discerned at Horton, Long Grove and West Park. The semicircular central corridor now forms the main route through the estates. A glance at a modern Ordnance Survey map still shows traces of the outlines you can see in the aerial photographs below.

After Enoch Powell's 1961 speech, water towers came to symbolise all that was wrong with the asylum system. Although the water towers at Horton and Long Grove were demolished, those at St Ebba's and West Park remain, and have been converted into desirable homes, with great views of the surrounding area. They are shown before closure on pages 95 and 96.

Above: The Manor Hospital, now Manor Park estate.

Left: Horton Hospital, now Livingstone Park. Much of the original landscaping remains. Horton, as the most exposed of the sites, was surrounded by tall poplars to act as windbreaks, as can be seen in this photograph. Some of these still exist in Long Grove Park near the playground.

Above: St Ebba's
Hospital, now Parkviews.

Right: Long Grove
Hospital, now
Clarendon Park.

West Park Hospital, now Noble Park. Poplars also surround this site.

The main administration building was at the centre of hospital life, with corridors and wards radiating from it. It contained offices, boardrooms and accommodation for senior medical staff. Probably because of the additional effort that was put into their design, the exterior of these blocks has survived largely unchanged and, extensively remodelled as apartments, they are now at the heart of the new estates. This is the building at Horton before its closure and remodelling as Balfour House. Note the water tower behind it and the distinctive yellow bricks in which much of the hospital was built, made from clay dug on the site.

Long Grove's imposing main building, now Prospect House, before closure.

St Ebba's main building, on a smaller scale and with elements of the popular Arts and Crafts style. This reflected the more domestic architecture of the villas arranged around a village green in what was originally designed as a 'colony' for people with epilepsy, which was considered a psychiatric illness at the turn of the century. The hospital later served those with learning disabilities.

Above: The original Horton Manor house served as the administration block for the Manor Asylum, and is shown here before closure. It was substantially rebuilt before being converted into apartments, but the distinctive red brick and parts of the original design remain.

Below: The central power station on Horton Lane, now a David Lloyd leisure centre. Service tunnels ran to each of the hospitals, and heating and electricity were supplied centrally for reasons of economy.

Above: Ward blocks were converted into luxury apartments at Horton, Long Grove and West Park. The West Park site retains the largest number of these blocks, as the hospital was built last and the condition of the buildings was better than on other sites. This is the infirmary building at Long Grove. Note the airing shelter in the foreground, provided so patients could benefit from fresh air in all weathers. Some of these have been retained at West Park, although they were demolished elsewhere.

Below: West Park airing shelter after closure.

Above: This Long Grove ward block, shown after closure, has the red brick and banding that can still be seen at Hunter and Harvey Court.

Below: Long Grove and Horton had a number of distinctive lodges at their various entrances on Horton Lane, which are now private homes.

St Ebba's water tower.

West Park water tower.